better to have lost.

Bekah Stogner

better to have lost.

Bekah Stogner

better to have lost
Copyright©2019 Bekah Stogner
All Rights Reserved
Published by Unsolicited Press
Printed in the United States of America.
First Edition 2019.

All rights reserved. Printed in the United States of America. No part of this book may be used or reproduced in any manner whatsoever without written permission except in the case of brief quotations embodied in critical articles or reviews.

Attention schools and businesses: for discounted copies on large orders, please contact the publisher directly.

For information contact:
Unsolicited Press
Portland, Oregon
www.unsolicitedpress.com
orders@unsolicitedpress.com
619-354-8005

Cover Design:
Editor: S.R. Stewart

ISBN: 978-1-947021-83-9

Table of Contents

deadroses.	9
death.	10
my grandfather died five years too late.	12
when my aunt died.	14
a poet.	16
reality.	17
reality II.	18
reality III.	19
open casket.	20
reality IV.	22
reality V.	23
in the confines of my soul.	24
lullaby.	25
cockroach.	26
sleep.	28
you and all your frailties.	29
wordswordswords.	30

for my mom.

deadroses.

A dead rose sits on the dashboard of my car.
I guess it reminds me to never hold onto anything for
        too long.
I guess it reminds me of the potential of beauty
and love
and happiness
and how quickly they can wither away
when loved too much.
I guess it reminds me that too much of a good thing
can kill you just the same.

death.

I have never seen anything die.
But I have seen what death can do.
I have seen a person crawling so close to the edge
of the cliff of never coming back,
each one of their meek breaths
feels more like a question.
I have seen my father weep.
I have watched the slow descent into derangement
with the rise of the medical bills
and I have seen the shock
and the numbness and the pain
and the way the world
just
stops.
But I have never cried for it.
I have stayed as far away from death as I could manage.
In those final days
I am nowhere to be seen.
As soon as the word
"death"
flies from the lips of those I love,
I vanish.
I run.
Death is not a hand I want to shake
skeletal fingers and the cigarettes on her breath
forming patterns in my thoughts
and telling me I don't really know
anything.

I have no authority to speak of death
I wouldn't go near when they were dying
yet, when I color my mind with constant
"What If"s
death is the first paint I reach for.
I have never seen anything die
but
I speak of death

like I am the reaper herself.

my grandfather died five years too late.

My grandfather's body tried to call it quits
so many times
crawled to the edge of the ring
bruised
bloodied
pumped full of pills
trying
to ring the bell and finally end the fight.
He fainted when he got his first tattoo
but somehow lived through lung cancer

His body was a warrior
His soul was a soldier
fighting a war we always knew he would lose.
It was just a matter of when.
When his skeleton took up residence with us
I watched you
and all of your hours
every ounce of your sweat
and everything that you were
vanish
into his gaping chasm of a mouth
his open wound of a body
his empty shell of a fatherhood.
I watched you disappear
into medicine patches
and oxygen tanks

and the constant anxiety of
when, when, when.
His ghost commanded our home.
His shallow breathing became the beating of our hearts
I had no choice.
Every day became the day.
Every second became the last.
I ran four hours away,
got drunk on cheap vodka and soda
slept poorly on a couch half the size of my body
just to get away from my home
that had become a sideshow of illness
a gallery of mourning.
A PowerPoint presentation on the stages of dying.
Here's where large bruises turn his paper skin a
        translucent purple.
Click.
Here's when he felt the best he's felt in years.
Click.
Here's where I ran four hours back home
only to stumble into his last moments
that I had intended to be so far away from
and still tell people that
someone has died in my house
to give them a good scare
when the only one who's still scared is me.
Click.

when my aunt died.

it was just another Monday morning.
I hated myself for not being able to wrap my arms
around my mother
when she wept in the living room of my apartment.
As normal as any other day.
I thought about what next Christmas might be like
without her terrible gifts
but we thanked her so much
before we threw the box away
and re-gifted the chunky necklaces and socks to our
friends.
It was a little cloudy, but not too cold.
I thought of how her life expectancy was already so
short and
wasn't she already a miracle?
I went to class.
Are you even supposed to be sad for someone who
didn't want to be alive anyway?
I went to work.
I don't believe in heaven anymore.
I went home.
I found the sporting goods gift card she had given me
crumpled at the bottom of my bag. It wasn't
her handwriting, but it was her message
a terrible gift
"I love you".

I laughed at her choice
I was never athletic
A different aunt, while handing me twelve crumpled
        ones
in exchange for the gift card
said
Maybe you should hang onto it,
just to laugh.
Just to laugh.
I became flooded with emotion that beat at the walls of
        my lungs
I wanted to cry
I wanted to scream
I wanted to tell someone
but no one would have understood.
I still can't process death
at the ripe old age of twenty one.
I can't stress enough how normal of a day it was.

a poet.

I don't have much to offer besides words
and even those are not enough.
I don't know how to react to terrible pain and suffering

without forcing a joke
discomforting, disingenuous laughter
or writing down the all the ways I feel
in some oversaturated letter.
I don't know what to say or do.
I don't know what's going to happen tomorrow.
I feel unsafe in my own skin.
I feel unloved in my being
in the things I cannot control,
but what can I do besides love others in return?
Today is hard, tomorrow may be harder.
This is the only way I know to cope.

reality.

I don't believe the mind can process the concept
of the reality
of death.
We can never accept a person as "gone".
After the initial shock of the loss, we wake up each
        morning
believing
they are still with us
calling out their name
only to remember
and
our body shuts down again
because we cannot fathom
the reality
of death
when our head creates dreams
sweet lies
that say otherwise.

reality II.

Once we have remembered how to walk and how to talk and how to live
without tears lining our eyes
we can never accept this person as "gone".
They're still here.
They're with us in the house.
They're in that gentle breeze that pulls at your jacket.
They're in that picture frame that keeps falling off the wall all because of a bent nail
but don't tell that to
anyone who's grieving
don't fix the nail
Don't try to pick up the pieces.
Leave the glass on the floor.
It's a message, after all.

reality III.

They're watching over us with a smile
they're in the stars
they're wherever we scattered
the burnt remains of them.
They're softly reminding us
about the cleanliness of their kitchen
or the right way to do
everything

everything
means
something.
Life means laughing with friends after midnight
and searching the sky
for the only constellation you know
and beauty
and breathing
but death?
This bullshit has to mean something.
It has to.
Doesn't it?

open casket.

A snake's venom kills slowly
it's hard to throw four years of anything away.
Your heart keeps beating, just slower
you're still technically alive
still holding on tight to the embers of something that was
or maybe it was always a facade.
Everyone else has already burnt their houses down.
Maybe I'm just too stuck on the idea of unconditionality
to save myself from burning alive
with two bite marks
dripping blood on my wrist
from when I offered out my hands
to save you.
You pass me
as if I don't exist
as if I were already the corpse
I dreamed of being.
Not a word not a word.
But you couldn't have forgotten
your murderous heartbreaks
how I held your head in my hands
two hours of tear-stained fabric between us.
You couldn't have forgotten
when you sent a distant cry for help
and I burst through the unlocked door
to hide all the kitchen knives.
People don't forget when they are immensely loved,

do they?
I hated and I loved you all at once.
How can you pass
the open casket of my bed
without so much placing a flower in between my scarred
fingertips
when I would've buried you in blooms?
How can you be so careless
when I both love and hate you still
but choose not to let go
of the kitchen knives?
They have not lowered me into the earth just yet.
Speak while you can.

reality IV.

Even when people around us begin to
die,

as the reaper drags
her skeletal fingers across the roots of our lives
we cannot accept that death is something that can
        happen to us
to those we love.
When someone you barely knew fades away
they're gone
good riddance
I'm sorry for your loss
so so sorry
but the world keeps spinning.
My mother asked me one day what I would do if my
        father died in his sleep one night.
I didn't even know what to say.

reality V.

I think about death at least once a day
every time my chest rises and falls
every time someone I love falls asleep
and I place my hand near their face to make sure
they are still with me
I think about death
but the fact that they will leave
and the fact that I don't know when
is something I can't seem to process.
These don't seem like things that could ever happen
until, of course
they do.
And then we cannot process the concept.
And sometimes we never accept the reality.
Denial, anger, bargaining, depression, acceptance
but do we ever accept death?
We accept that spirits keep us company
we accept that we will, one day,
be reunited somehow
but we do not
cannot
accept
the reality of death
as she exists
as she presents herself
to us mortals.
Somehow, I understand
that we are not meant to.

in the confines of my soul.

You can hear a pin drop
in the hollowness of the walls.

lullaby.

Put me to sleep with
a gentle rock and a soft forehead kiss
Remember when you said you loved me?
It feels like so long ago
we laughed and smiled
my joyous knees shaking,
but I hardly stopped to notice.
Three weeks feels like ten years to me.
Put me to sleep
I cannot cry out
my throat is trying to close
I think my body is trying to shut you out
while my mind holds onto you dearly
runs its fingers through your hair
grabs the ends and pulls.
You are mine.
You were mine.
You are no longer mine.
Put me to sleep with your sweet voice
that has turned so cold
I'll just put on a sweater
whatever it takes to be here with you.
Put me to sleep.
I am nothing without you.

cockroach.

The dreams about you
are an unwelcome cockroach
crawling from my unsuspecting thoughts
into the deepest parts of my brain,
racking the walls with wishes long forgotten
and details I must fill in myself,
creating this image of you that I never really knew.
The cockroach crawls into my heart
waking me up with a gasp
and burrowing deep where it hurts
the most.
I taste you for the rest of the day.
I hear that idealistic version of you
speaking in my ear.
I tremble with my imagined happiness.
For two long years now,
I have been roaming around
the confines of your fever dream,
heart sweltering with your promise
the flames of your fingertips
the blazing idea that no conversation I've had since
can ever hold a candle
to you
to yours
to your words and ideas.

Everyone I meet sounds like
a watered-down version
of your red wine words
and my tongue is stained red
from the constant talking.
The thing about a cockroach that's gone missing
is that it never really dies.
It wanders the walls of the body
day after day
scattering along the synapses
reminding me of that poem you wrote
and showed to me at 2AM.
The one I've never been able to forget.
It reminds me how long it's been
since I let it loose in my heart
and how long I've been unable
to let you go.

sleep.

My hands are chained to sleep's loving
deceiving embrace.
She keeps me captive but I do not see
my life slipping away
How can I?
My eyes are closed and my mind unawake

you and all your frailties.

your eyelashes like snowflakes
soft on your face
sleeping in the next room over
saying you're so sad
yet you are so unaware.
Sadness muddles the most beautiful eyes
and holds your heart down
with the strength of a thousand burdens.
She kills innocence like monsters
and holds you hostage with her venomous possessions
of sleep
keeping you awake for ages sometimes
never letting you rise.
These are the things that I have known.
You may say you're sad
my love
and I'll kiss your eyelashes and
keep you safe like I always have
but you have never known
how it truly feels

wordswordswords.

I wish I could take back
every word I've ever said
that might have made you think
even for a moment
that I was angry with you.
I wish I could take all the words
that ever hurt you
and swallow them
like daggers in my own stomach
just so you would have no reason to
remember me as anything but
your angel
when you leave.

About the Author

Bekah Stogner recently graduated from Lipscomb University in Nashville, Tennessee with a BA in Writing and a BFA in Acting, where she co-created *Poetry Night*. Bekah remains active in the Nashville theatre, improv, and poetry communities and hopes to continue to pursue both editing and acting. *better to have lost* is her first collection of poetry.

About the Press

Unsolicited Press was founded in 2012 and is based Portland, Oregon. The team is comprised of volunteers and seeks to produce stunning poetry, fiction, and creative nonfiction.

Learn more at www.unsolicitedpress.com.

www.ingramcontent.com/pod-product-compliance
Lightning Source LLC
Chambersburg PA
CBHW030136100526
44591CB00009B/685